O
SLIVER
OF
LIVER

O
SLIVER
OF
LIVER

Together with other triolets,
cinquains, haiku, verses
and a dash of poems

by MYRA COHN LIVINGSTON

drawings by Iris Van Rynbach

A MARGARET K. MC ELDERRY BOOK

Atheneum 1979 *New York*

In Memory of My Father

Mayer Louis Bud Cohn

August 21, 1896
November 10, 1977

811.54
J L/ V

Library of Congress Cataloging in Publication Data

Livingston, Myra Cohn.
  O sliver of liver.

  "A Margaret K. McElderry book."
  SUMMARY: More than 40 poems covering such topics as nature, holidays, daily life, human relationships, and emotions.

  [1. American Poetry] I. Title.
PZ8.3.L75 Oac   811'.5'4   78-21190
ISBN 0-689-50133-1

CONTENTS

An Angry Valentine

If you won't be my Valentine
I'll *scream*, I'll *yell*, I'll *bite!*
I'll cry aloud, I'll start to whine
If you won't be my Valentine.
I'll frown and fret, I'll mope and whine,
And it will serve you right—
If you won't be my Valentine
I'll *scream*, I'll *yell*, I'll *bite!*

Argument

How the birds quarrel
among themselves this morning
over one small worm!

Bird Talk

Whatever you have
to say, mockingbird, tell it
to me in a hurry—

the bluejays want a moment
to squawk me their own brash songs!

Chambered Nautilus

Larger,
   larger
      they grow, my rooms of
         sloping pearl walls,
            ceilings,
               floors;

I glide from one   to   another.

I am leaving the womb,
        the small rooms
           where I began

Winding my way toward the
                            tangled kelp,
                the
                    swelling

            of the colored world.

Larger,
   larger
      I grow, bringing with me

               a marvel for them to see—
            the wonder I have made of my

             chambered nautilus.

Driveway

One long crack in the
pavement . . . . an endless freeway
for commuting ants.

February 14

I love you nearly *all* the time
But mostly when it's Spring;
So when it comes I make a rhyme,
"*I love you* nearly all the time."
But now I need a Valentine
And you're the closest thing.
I love you *nearly* all the time—
But mostly when it's Spring.

For Sara

Every flower should have a friend—

For the pansy, a cutworm,
For the calla lily, a snail,
For impatience, a hummingbird,
For the poppy, a nibbling rabbit,
For the camellia, a family of ants,

And for the rose, me.

Forest Fire

Red sun,
smothered in smoke
from raging forest fires,
black ashes are weeping over
our earth.

Red sun,
call forth the rain.
Let it pour from gray clouds,
drown the orange fire tongues, dry all
our tears.

Red sun,
you who are lord,
summon the storms; turn ash
to dust. Shine through blue sky. Smile
yellow.

Garden

Who has the better
right to smell the first summer
rose, bee—you or I?

A Ghostly Conversation

Smell me,
I rise from rotten ground . . .

                                        NO

Taste me,
I am all cold, black air . . .

                                        NO

Touch me,
I have no bones, no hair . . .

                                        NO

Look at me,
My sunken eyes, my transparent shroud . . .

                                        NO

Listen to me,
Wailing, crying, calling to *you* . . .

                                        NO

Be with me, then,
Allhallow's Eve,
Be with me, pity me,
I have no friend but you . . .

Be with me . . .   NO

B o o o o o o o o o o o o o o o o o o o

Go Away

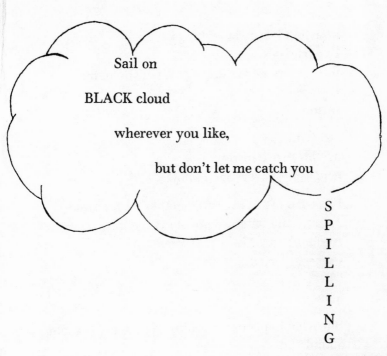

Sail on

BLACK cloud

wherever you like,

but don't let me catch you

S
P
I
L
L
I
N
G

R
A
I
N

on

me

I Haven't Learned to Whistle

I haven't learned to whistle.
I've tried—
But if there's anything like a whistle in me,
It stops
Inside.

Dad whistles.
My brother whistles
And almost everyone I know.

I've tried to put my lips together with wrinkles,
To push my tongue against my teeth
And make a whistle
Come
Out
Slow—

But what happens is nothing but a feeble gasping
Sound
Like a sort of sickly bird.

(Everybody says they never heard
A whistle like *that*
And to tell the truth
Neither did I.)

But Dad says, tonight, when he comes home,
He'll show me again how
To put my lips together with wrinkles,
To push my tongue against my teeth,
To blow my breath out and really make a whistle,

And I'll *try!*

Idea

I have
planted two seeds
in the ground, to sprout up,
grow tall, blossom together and
be friends!

January

Here we are, Winter,
just you and I in the snow
freezing together.

Kitchen Thought

Little
brown cloves, they have
stolen you from far-off
lands to stir in their kettles of
dinner.

Will you
swim around and
season their boiling shrimp?
let them grind you for flavoring
their cakes?

No! Don't!
Just whisper to
your friend cloves . . . "Let's escape
and run back home on our four short
brown legs!"

Lights: Cambridge, Massachusetts

I'm putting you into a poem, lights,
Shining yellow-blue across the Charles River,
A slippery path of wet pebbles
Leading to Boston.

Square eyes
Green/slant/eyes
You squint at me   patterned   like
                       building blocks

              another
           above
        one
      stacked

      running in twos   in fo ur s
             in twos   in fo ur s

      two little pairs of eyes
      scuttle past
      and then   two more
                 two more
                 two more

You make rivers within rivers,
Black patches,
Long thin ghosts without feet
Undulating in the water   dancing

No one could paint this picture
And make it true   but
I'm putting you into a poem, lights,
To shine forever in my head.

little o

little
o, the earth, bathed
in ocean, how bravely
you tumble through the black nothing
of space

Mad Song

I shut my door
To keep you out
Won't do no good
To stand and shout
Won't listen to
A thing you say
Just time you took
Yourself away
I lock my door
To keep me here
Until I'm sure
You disappear

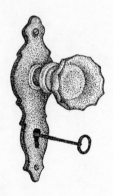

Making a Friend

He wouldn't come at first.
But when
I stood quite still a long time,
Then

His tail began to move.
His eyes
Looked into mine, and in
Surprise

He sort of sniffed and showed
His tongue.
Then, suddenly, he moved and
Sprung

To where I stood. He smelled
My feet
And came up close so we could
Meet.

So then, I gently stroked
His head.
"Good boy—I'll be your friend,"
I said.

He licked me then, and that
Was good,
Because it meant
He understood.

Never

Never tell a secret to
        a snoopy whatchacallit who
        will whisper it in sneaky tones
        on surreptitious telephones
        so anyone who listens hears
        embroideries within their ears
        and adds some little gobs of guile
        and bits of bosh and flimflam smile

        so when it travels back to you
        it's changed so much you'll think it's *true!*

New Year's Eve

We got a broom (like Father said)
And just before we went to bed

We opened up the cold back door
And swept the old year out before

We ran to let the New Year in
The front, and told him to begin

And blew our horns and gave a shout
To see the old year running out!

O Sliver of Liver

O sliver of liver,
Get lost! Go away!
You tremble and quiver
O sliver of liver—
You set me a-shiver
And spoil my day—
O sliver of liver,
Get lost! Go away!

Parched Earth

For Sarah Reed

Prying into each crack
I will lift out the jigsaw-puzzle ground
Piece   by   piece.

Carefully, I will push the pieces aside.
Silently, I will descend
                    down
                            down
                                    down.

No one will know I am gone.
No one will know where I am.
No one will know what I have seen.

When I return
I will fit the jigsaw puzzle together
Piece   by   piece.

All that will remain are the cracks.

In time

            the grass

                                            too.
                            these

            will cover

Piano Lesson (Carissa)

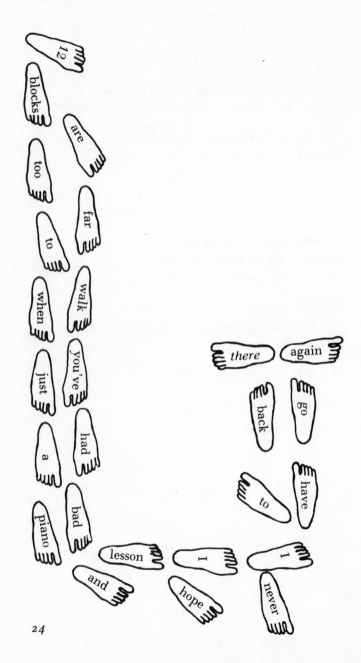

A Question

Ocean, how do you
know when to curve and make of
the earth a round ball?

Sack Lunch

Tuna sandwich
  in my lunch;
Celery and sprouts
  to munch;
Pickles,
Cookies,
Apricot—
But where's my napkin?

            You forgot!!!

A Sad Valentine

O Valentine, it's such a shame
That you and I are through.
'Twas sheer delight to call your name—
O Valentine, it's such a shame
But heaven knows, *I'm* not to blame.
It surely must be *you*.
O Valentine, it's such a shame
That you and I are through.

School Thoughts

School's over at last!
Even the birds are chirping
with sounds of laughter!

The first day of school—
does my teacher wonder who
these new faces are?

Sea Level Drive

For Ruth Greenberg

Today is the day of
    a beach holiday
    where the line of the earth
    against sky   melts away

    and what was an ocean
    is only the sky
    and sky turns to yellow
    and frothing waves fly

    to the sailing clouds over
    and up to the sun
    where the blinding gold
    flashlight of noon has begun

    to flick from the top
    and come dancing away
    striking the waves
    in a glint of the spray

    where yellow and blue
    meet in curling white hands
    shining green for a second
    and bathing the sands

    and the belt of the earth
    loosens low and away

    and the sky floods with yellow
    and this is   *my* day.

Small Song

Telephone lines, look
how the birds turn you into
a musical staff!

Somewhere Between Utah and Nevada: Airborne

Mountains, melting off cold snow,
Watched when standing from below,
Weave icy streams that wind and flow.

> Airborne, here they crouch and lie
> Clustered below the height of sky;
> Hulking torsos left to die.

> Black-ribbed bodies, bleached-white bone,
> Stretching far to graves unknown,
> Nameless, naked and alone;

> Ancient birds, struck down in flight,
> Armadillos, stiff with fright,
> Giant turtles, killed by night.

Who sees them on the ground beneath
Knows only snow; no tears, no grief.
The moon stares down in disbelief.

Storyteller

For Siddie Joe Johnson

> "I did not see a mermaid . . ."

I
Mermaids
you made . . . rising
from a sandy gulf coast,
washing them into the Story
Hour.

II
They dive
among us . . . scales
and golden hair tangle,
shimmer, comb through waves and swells to
your chair.

III
Their tails
beat in rhythm
to your voice . . . and children—
even we, who never believed—
hear them.

IV

You say,
"I did not see—"
We laugh, for we know the
sun had blinded your eyes for a
moment.

V

They swim
into our lives . . .
they cannot return to
their sea . . . they make salt sting hard on
our lips.

T-Shirt

T-shirt,
you're my best thing
though you've faded so much
no one knows what you said when you
were new.

To a Turkey

Gobble
your last sad gasp,
for tomorrow, turkey,
your head chopped off, your feathers plucked,
you will

be stuffed,
cooked crispy brown
and brought to the table
where we will bow our heads in thanks
for you,

turkey,
giver of the
Thanksgiving feast . . . Cheer up!
Who else but you, at this dinner,
is king?

To Orion

Your belt
is made of stars,
Orion—how did you
buckle them up together so
brightly?

Your sword
is brilliant specks
of white gold—when did you
carry it up so high to your
sky forge?

Your home
in the dark is
where I look, Orion,
for I wish to be as clever
as you!

Umbrellas

Small colored tents
pop up above people's heads
at the first raindrop.

Views from Trancas Beach

Now that the fishing
boat has left, sea gulls know where
to find their dinner!

For one instant, a
green curving wall, and then a
burst of white ruffles.

Slowly the ocean
sucks in its breath, letting it
out with a gurgle.

Squawk at the ocean,
sea gulls; it will still roar out
much louder than you.

How angry you are
today, ocean, as your waves
knock me off my feet!

No matter how hard
the waves push, the kelp beds stay
anchored in ocean.

Warrior

In silver armor,
the lizard, felled by rain, dreams
of his summer sun.

What My Bed Says

You squirm and settle down in me
when the day goes.
I feel the ends of your toes
naked and free
from shoes and socks, and I cover
all the laughter and tears of your day.
Here in my snug world you stay,
and the dreams we discover
in the dark patterns of the night
make us feel as one.
Then comes another sun,
and its first light
tears us apart, for you wake and turn
from me, battered, wrinkled, in folds.
Leave then—see what the day holds
and share it with me when you return.

Wind: A Cinquain Sequence

Wind through
the half-opened
window whispers angry
arguments of two wizened old
people.

Wind at
the seashore skims
the sand, stirs the sandflies,
shoots shivers of coolness through
my skin.

Hot wind
on a summer
day scorches my ears, my
neck and chases me into dark
cool shade.

Spring wind
sings the promise
of melting snow, pale sun
and a place to play outdoors
barefoot.

Winter Tree

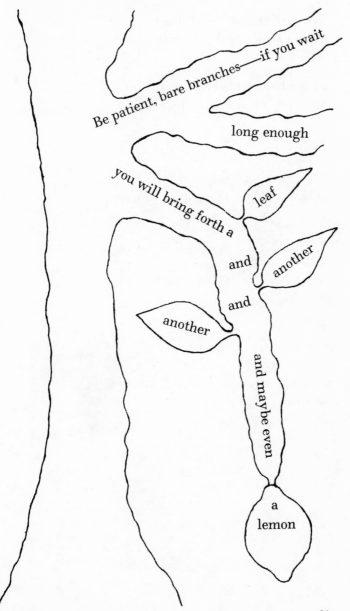

Be patient, bare branches—if you wait
long enough
you will bring forth a
leaf
and
another
and
another
and maybe even
a
lemon

Wonder

What mermaid found this
yellow scallop shell, waved
it as a sea fan,

dressed herself in white coral
and bewitched a green merman?